Hello Hello

Written by Fumiko Takeshita
Illustrated by Jun Takabatake

Kane/Miller
BOOK PUBLISHERS

It used to be, we could only speak
face to face.

Later on, we could write letters.

But now, we have
telephones.
"Hello, hello!"
It's fast and easy.

"Hello, Grandma. Thank you for my birthday present."

We can talk to people no matter where they are.

For emergencies,
when we need to
report a fire,

or call the police,
we just dial 911.
The telephone can
be very helpful.

It can also be helpful when we're hungry.

For business,

or pleasure,

in the country,

or in the city, we can use
the telephone.

Telephone calls can be short or long.

Early in the morning,

very late at night,

during bath time,

or in the middle of dinner,
the telephone might ring.

All over the world,
people use the telephone.

Maybe in the future,
we'll get a call from
somewhere else.
How will we answer?

"Hello, this is Earth."

"Hello, hello."